DOWNLOAD THE WORKBOOK AND AUDIOBOOK FREE!

I've found readers have the most success with this book when they use the workbook as they read.

So to thank you for your purchase of *Break Your Bad Love Habits* I'd like to give you the workbook 100% free.

Go to emilyrosecoaching.com/byblh-workbook to download now!

BREAK YOUR BAD LOVE HABITS:

5 Steps to Free Yourself from Heartbreak and Transform Your Relationships Forever

EMILY ROSE

Second Edition
ISBN-10: 1508546150
ISBN-13: 978-1508546153

Design: Ida Fia Sveningsson
Editor: Katherine Miller

DEDICATION

This book is dedicated to you, lovely reader
—my inspiration for why I do what I do. Because you desire to be
your best self—because you know that by being your best self you
help not only yourself, but also the world around you—
I dedicate this book to you.

TABLE OF CONTENTS

ACKNOWLEDGMENTS

There are so many people—too many to name here—who have given me deeper insight into myself through our time together in relationships, be they friends, family, or romantic partners. Without those mirrors to help me peer into my inner self, I would not have the capacity to share what I have learned and to help guide others on their paths of inner peace, love, and joy.

I want to give a special thank you to Nolan Tatro, without whom this book would never have been written; to my mom, Lainie Turner, my ultimate rock and biggest supporter; to my brother and bestie, Coleman Howard; to CaliCat, my precious girl and faithful companion of sixteen years; to my dear friend Christopher Waterbury, for his undying support and encouragement in my journey of life; to my oldest friend and muse Amanda Madraso, for inspiring the creation of many of the tools and techniques found in this book; to my beloved girlfriend, Beth Petta, for her love, light, insight, time, and true friendship; to my generous and talented editor, Katherine Miller; to my incredible designer, Ida Fia Sveningsson; to Self-Publishing School; to my wonderful coach, friend, mentor, and spirit sister, Bev Adamo; and to my most beloved Team Changemakers—the whole lot—with a deep appreciation and extremely special thanks to Melissa Smith, Suzy Milhoan, Amber Brogly, Jaime Grodberg, Emily Ann Peterson, Cary Hokama, and Cindy Starke.

I wouldn't be where I am without the support and strength each of you has brought to me in different ways, throughout the process of writing and relaunching this book, and throughout my life.

Thank you.

INTRODUCTION

Whether you are single, in a relationship, or carrying the "it's complicated" status in your head, heart, or on Facebook, the lessons in this book will give you insight into the bad habits you are unconsciously bringing into romantic relationships.

Tell me if any of this sounds familiar . . .

When in a romantic relationship, you feel stifled, suffocated, and totally lacking in freedom. You're used to "losing" yourself in relationships, which is why you're either struggling with a romantic relationship right now or apprehensive about getting back into one.

Perhaps you "relationship hop." You jump from one relationship to the next without giving yourself time in between to do the inner work necessary to evolve as an individual and stay strong in that individuality within a romantic relationship.

Perhaps at this point you're so exhausted by relationships that you're just about ready to give up on the notion that your dream partner really exists, but somewhere inside of you is that nagging feeling that you know they're out there and that you're meant to meet them.

Or maybe you've met them. Maybe you're in a relationship that you don't necessarily want to leave, but it's driving you bananas. All you want is to learn a few tricks to inspire change in your partner and live a more self-defined life, free to be your whole, awesome self.

Or maybe you're simply ready for a break from relationships altogether. Maybe enough is enough and you're just ready to have some simple solution to these complex problems plop itself right down in your lap in an easily digestible format. While no single book or program can fully cover the vast array of human beings' interpersonal relationships, this is a book that will address the fundamental issues and dynamics holding you back from healthy, happy romantic relationships.

Break Your Bad Love Habits delivers compact, well-defined solutions to love's most pressing issues. Diving into the heart of both the pleasant and unpleasant realities of romantic relationships, this book offers perspective and advice unlike any other. This book is for those who are tired of repeating the same unsuccessful relationship cycles, who have tried everything and seem to fall back into the same situations over and over again, and who want those elusive "ah ha" moments without spending years in therapy.

After studying and implementing thousands of techniques in my own life and relationships, I've helped countless people break free from unwanted relationship patterns, find their voices, and step fully into their authentic selves, and from that place of self-love and self-acceptance create their dream-come-true realities and relationships.

Known by many as The Breakup Coach, I've explored the nuances of balancing the masculine and feminine roles within the self and within romantic relationships, allowing individuals to reclaim their independence, live more self-defined lives, and learn the very important art of deep and abiding self-trust. Through the lessons in this book, you'll gain a whole new set of tools that will help you simply and swiftly deal with the ups and downs of singlehood and romantic partnership. Whether you're looking to manage arguments better, have a more fulfilling sex life with your long term partner, or understand the psychology of the all-too-typical push-pull dynamic of modern relationships, this book is for you.

Let this book open your eyes to the transformation that occurs when you are willing to bring to your consciousness the ways in which you might be compromising the integrity of your relationships—and then take action on that enlightenment and be willing to look at the not-so-attractive parts of your inner being.

As you read on, you'll hear about some of the experiences that allowed me to shift from incessantly breaking hearts and being heartbroken to having successful romantic relationships.

I'll share with you specific steps that will help you completely transform your relationship to relationships.

When you take the time to self-reflect and own the ways in which you affect your environment, you then have the power to shape your reality and relationships into exactly what you want them to be. Albert Einstein said it best: "No problem can be solved from the same level of consciousness that created it."

Albert Einstein is right, and it's up to you to decide how much longer you're willing to turn a blind eye to these simple solutions and stay unsure, unsatisfied, and underappreciated.

Break Your Bad Love Habits presents familiar scenarios and gives clear, actionable steps for creating the best dynamic possible in (and out of) romantic relationships. As you focus on your inner self, raising your self-awareness and practicing self-love and self-acceptance, all of your relationships will shift from shallow and precarious to deep and expansive in love, trust, and authenticity.

If you implement the simple, easy-to-understand concepts in this book, I promise you will find more fulfillment not only in your romantic relationships, but also in your friendships, your familial relationships, and most importantly, your relationship with yourself. I promise that by following the exercises and practices in each section, you *will* experience a deeper sense of self-trust that will give you the ability to have more authentic, loving relationships than ever before, and ultimately to call in your ideal partner and relationship.

But you must implement these exercises and follow through with the practices. As legendary author Jack Canfield said:

> "Everything you want also wants you.
> But you have to take action to get it."

It's time to stop repeating the same unfulfilling, unsuccessful relationship patterns. It's time to become aware of a new way of being in relationships and being with yourself. It's time to stop wearing different masks and being different versions of yourself with different people in your life—it's time to stand up and be YOU.

All you need to do is keep reading to learn the most common pitfalls of romantic relationships and what you can do to save yourself and others a whole lot of heartache and heartbreak.

Discover these new strategies to old problems right now and use them to create your dream-come-true romantic relationship.

HOW TO

BREAK

YOUR BAD

LOVE

HABITS

How to Break
Your Bad Love Habits

For years I walked around letting life happen to me, and in that time I cycled through romantic relationship after romantic relationship. I actually came up with the term "relationship hopping" because that's exactly what I did—jumping out of one relationship and into the next one without any time in between to process, reflect, or grow.

Finally, in 2007 I had a heartbreak that was bad enough to wake me up and make me realize I had a choice in who I was in this life and how I was going to live.

After years of deep self-work, my perspective on life changed dramatically. I wasn't just freed from my unwanted relationship patterns; I was also freed from my scarcity mindset in all aspects of life. I wound up traveling the world for two and a half years, living in Maui, Costa Rica, and touring Panama, Vietnam, Japan, and parts of the United States. In fact, it was in Costa Rica that I met my life-changing soul partner, and it's thanks to him and our time together I can be here with you today, sharing the lessons I've learned when it comes to creating a rich, fulfilling, successful romantic relationship.

Below you'll find a breakdown of exactly how to break your bad love habits, just like I did.

Step 1. Reclaim Your Joy: Make Your Mind Work for You
Step 2. Shift Your Perspective: See the True Love in Your Life
Step 3. Clear the Past: Close Doors to Open More
Step 4. Receive Love: Understand the Patterns and Break the Habits
Step 5. Manifest Consciously: Attract Your Dream Relationship NOW

While it will be tempting to just read or listen to the exercises and think, "Yeah, I could see that being really helpful," *not* taking action and completing these transformative practices will guarantee that you will continue the same unwanted relationship cycles. So if you really want to break your bad love habits—and I believe you do, since you purchased this book and have read this far already—then for the sake of healthy, loving relationships with yourself and others, complete the workbook, make the practices a part of your daily life, and watch your entire reality become your dream reality.

Ancient Roman philosopher Seneca said, "Luck is what happens when preparedness meets opportunity."

You bought this book because you are prepared to make changes, and this book is your opportunity to do so.

Follow through with the exercises as they're set forth, and watch yourself become extraordinarily lucky in life and in love.

STEP 1
Reclaim Joy: Make Your Mind Work for You

If you haven't already noticed, your mind is *super* powerful. What you think determines how you feel, act, and engage with others. If you're kind to yourself, you'll likely be kind to others, and if you're not-so-kind to yourself, you'll likely be not-so-kind to others as well. A positive attitude breeds a positive relationship, and while it's easy to conceptualize, implementing practices that shift one's perspective from lack and negativity to abundance and positivity can be a difficult task to accomplish without specific guidelines and tools to ease the process.

In order to transform your relationship to relationships, you need to do a few things. First, you have to neutralize self-judgment—discover the light side of the darkness, and view yourself with compassion. Next, you need to define exactly what you want in a partner, and then take the practice one step further—but not until you've thoroughly completed delineating the qualities you desire in your ideal partner. Finally, you need to go on a diet—a spiritual diet.

In this first step, you'll discover exercises and practices that take you through each of these prerequisites to reclaiming your joy and making your mind work for you.

It's easy to accept the bright, shiny, happy side of ourselves—the side we're proud of—but it's not so easy to acknowledge the dark side of ourselves, let alone accept it. To become aware of this darker self, also known as the shadow self, takes deep inner work.

Yet in order to create successful and fulfilling relationships with yourself and others, you must first learn how to deeply and completely accept your *whole* self, which includes both the light and the shadow.

The shadow self holds our shame—it holds resentment, grief, guilt, and the negative belief systems that lock us in unconscious patterns which result in unsuccessful relationships. Of course being in a romantic relationship can be challenging, because so often you're faced with the reality that you are not as loving, patient, or accepting as you once thought . . . or at least hoped. In fact, many people find it's a lot easier to leave a relationship and stop facing their stuff than it is to see it through and dare to stare into the heart of a gaping inner wound.

Getting to know and love another person can be pleasant, lovely, and sometimes even euphoric. Yet getting to know and love one's self can be painful, dark, and sometimes downright ugly. *But it must be done in order to heal wounds, neutralize emotional triggers, and cease undesirable patterns.*

In this chapter I offer a simple and effective technique that will help you to face your shadow self—the side of your being you'd rather deny exists altogether—and then accept it. And it's important to note that the more willing you are to become vulnerable with yourself, the more of yourself you'll come to accept. Because in order to live in a state of complete self-acceptance, we cannot deny that the dark parts exist.

Worksheet #1

I encourage you to do this exercise with pen and paper rather than on a device. There is something about writing by hand that allows thoughts to flow more freely.

> In the workbook, you'll find a worksheet called "Qualities I Do and Do Not Like About Myself." On one side of the sheet, write those of your qualities you'd rather deny exist altogether.

Think about the aspects of yourself you're not so proud of, the things you wish you could change or do better with in life. Complete this list before moving on to the next part of the exercise.

Now, on the opposing side of the sheet, acknowledge how these qualities manifest in ways you *do* like. Remember to consider how these qualities are an asset to your character, and recall instances where they've served you well.

Once you've completed both lists, close your eyes for a moment, relax, take a deep breath, then look at the exercise with fresh eyes. Consider it from a bigger perspective, and realize that every aspect of life has a sense of duality. For the sake of balance, everything has opposing energies. Really feel the ways in which the unwanted aspects of yourself do serve you at times. Hold appreciation for the benefits that counter the negative self-judgments. Finally, use this guide as a framework for which aspects of yourself you will nurture in the future, and which you will release.

This simple exercise helps you to release negative self-judgments and gives you the opportunity to neutralize the voice of your harsh inner critic. In doing so, you can learn to accept the parts of yourself you might typically try to hide or deny.

It is imperative to accept the darkness as well as the light in order to stand in your wholeness and live in full authenticity.

By learning to accept your *whole* self rather than just your pretty parts, you'll become more willing to get uncomfortable in romantic relationships and to sit with the experiences that bring you face to face with your shadow self. You'll also experience less discomfort in alone time, reducing your fear of loneliness and enabling you to enjoy your freedom more.

Of course, this is not intended to encourage anyone to stay in a relationship that is largely unenjoyable. Rather, it offers you the opportunity to use your self-judgments as a means of learning to love yourself more deeply, accept yourself more completely, and live from a place of true authenticity.

Exercise #1

From this place of deeper authenticity and vulnerability, reflect on the qualities you desire in your ideal partner.

Beyond the physical qualities, think about how they are with you, how they are with others, and how they are with themselves. Consider what they like—what makes them happy? What do they like to do? And on the other side of things, what don't they like— what makes them unhappy? What do they *not* like to do? Think of who and how they are in this world, and use the outline in the workbook entitled "What My Ideal Partner is Like" as a reference for completing the exercise.

In order to attract your ideal partner, you must first be *very* clear on the type of person you desire as a companion. The "Ideal Partner" worksheet covers the basics, but you're welcome to go beyond this and really dream up your ideal mate. Do know that even if you think you've got all your bases covered, your perfect partner will come with their own quirks. But the better you match on the important values, lifestyle choices, and future desires (as well as present behaviors), the less likely it is that those quirks will deter a long-term committed relationship.

Practice #1

To complete this first step and really reclaim your joy in life, you must go on a spiritual diet—a positivity diet.

Yes, I'm about to ask you to fast from cynicism, sarcasm, and gossip, and gorge on bliss.

Going on a positivity diet will change your life by changing your perspective, and unlike other diets this one does not need to be lifelong, though you may want it to be by the time you're done. The trick here is to go full out and not for a second allow negativity to seep in. If you adopt any practice from this entire book, make it this one. Go on a positivity diet for *a minimum of three months* and watch your entire world shift. You'll notice a difference in your mood during the first week. During the second week you'll notice how many people around you are stuck in negative thought-patterns. Beyond that, you'll begin to find yourself attracted to new, happy people, and from there you may begin to realize the joy in which you can reside for the rest (or at least the majority) of your life. Use the positivity diet chart in the workbook to record your mood shifts over the next three months.

Your new diet will consist of:

- **Comedies:** Movies, TV shows, YouTube clips—whatever you consume with your eyes, make it hilarious. Watch only funny things . . . or cute animal videos are cool, too.

- **Happy Music:** Listen to music that is upbeat and high-tempo with positive lyrics. Make sure what you're singing to yourself is funny, or simply fun. If Sarah McLaughlin makes you happy, at least omit her sullen tunes until after the diet's worked its magic.

- **Positive Conversations:** Like I said before, now is the time to quit gossiping. Gossip is poison transferring from one person to another via words. The next time you're talking to a friend and they begin to speak ill of another, see their words as thick, black mucous trying to make its way into your mouth—for if you consume that poison, you'll need to purge it as well, which usually involves passing it along to someone else. (Even if it's not the same gossip, the trend remains—best to refrain altogether.) Keep your convos happy, inspired, and full of love and support. This is also a great time to practice listening, but always feel free to redirect conversations to the positive when needed. You can even tell your friends about this diet and let them know talking negatively about others is a no-go for you from here on out.

Realize that all of your senses are absorbent. They are the medium through which you experience the world. Whatever you perceive with your eyes, nose, ears, mouth, or skin, you're inviting it into your inner world. And if you desire a positive, conscious, healthy outer world, you must maintain a positive, conscious, healthy inner world.

Once you have begun to neutralize self-judgment, you will be well on your way to having a compassionate relationship with yourself—one filled with love, acceptance, and inner peace. From here, by serving yourself a great big scoop of positivity, you can take that inner peace to both inward and outward places of joy. And while you work to call in a romantic relationship or reshape your current one, you can enjoy your time here on Earth. Neutralize your self-judgment, specify what you want in a partner, and then turn your attention to the positive. See how your life changes.

The next step to breaking your bad love habits and calling in a truly successful romantic relationship is to continue shifting your perspective. I know it seems like a lot to believe, but the way in which we perceive the world shapes the way in which the world responds to us—so it can either be awesome or miserable, depending on the eyes we're looking through.

This next step will solidify your newfound joyful perspective and bring your attention to the love that surrounds you in life. It will also show you the depths of some of your most fundamental obstacles where love is concerned and guide you in the final step in the ideal partner exercise.

STEP 2
Shift Your Perspective:
See the True Love in Your Life

Now that you've practiced neutralizing self-judgment, created the foundation for calling in your ideal partner, and committed to your new spiritual diet of positivity, it's time to come face to face with your unconscious self.

In this step, you will learn the details (and importance) of seeing yourself in others—how to use the world around you as a mirror to reveal the "good," the "bad," and the unconscious patterns that sabotage your relationships with yourself and others. You'll also come to understand that just as others are a reflection for you, you are a reflection for others, and it is important to respond to those reflections accordingly.

This chapter will give you exercises and practices that will help you make peace in your relationships (with friends, family, co-workers, and romantic partners); use your self-awareness to attract your ideal partner; and set in place regular gratitude practices that cradle your days in appreciation, ultimately helping you to shift your perspective and recognize the love in your life.

In order for you to create your ideal life and relationship, you must first realize that your outer world is a reflection of your inner world.

With so many facets to our inner selves, it's no wonder that we cannot see them all. Fortunately, by way of our judgments of others ("good" or "bad," "right" or "wrong"), we can peek beyond our conscious minds and into the beliefs that guide our actions, emotions, and thoughts.

You see, we all carry around belief systems that shape our perspectives—the ways in which we see the world around us. Just like our bodies need exercise, so do our perspectives. Stretching our belief systems and consciously choosing what we think and how we behave is part of becoming an awakened individual—part of choosing who and how we want to be in this world, rather than relying on old programming to dictate our relationships and self-identities.

But shifting your belief systems and expanding your perspective requires practice. The following exercise will help you to expand your self-awareness and facilitate more peaceful relationships with others in your life, reducing harsh judgments of others that keep you bound to negative mindsets, emotions, and thoughts.

Worksheet #2

Carve out some time to give this transformative process the attention it deserves. And be sure to use a pen and paper to facilitate a stream of consciousness and allow for the easy transcription of your natural flow of thoughts.

Bring to mind four people you have (or have had) a hard time accepting. These people should conjure feelings of fairly extreme emotions, ranging from tremendous frustration to vehement disapproval. You might simply not like the way these people are for no specific reason . . . or you might have a very specific reason. Either way, bring four people to mind who trigger negative emotions within you.

Now, using Worksheet #2, "Mirror Mirror in Another" found in the workbook, write the names of those people in the appropriate places. Under each name, list the qualities you find so unappealing in that person. The deeper you can go here, the better.

Once you have completed all that you can, stop for a moment to recalibrate. Sitting in such a state of discontent can be disconcerting, especially if you're on a positivity diet. So take it easy for a moment here. Shut your eyes, take some deep breaths, maybe burn some sage, and think about something awesome. Give yourself a moment, then continue on to the next page of the worksheet.

Now that you're operating from a less emotionally charged perspective, it's time to evaluate the similarities between each of the triggers you've listed. Perhaps you've found the same quality you despise under all four of the people, or maybe you've found that a few of them share similar traits that irk you. On the worksheet, list the similarities, and next to each similarity, write what it is about this quality that you do not like.

Finally, it's time to turn the mirror around. If you stay open and vulnerable here, you'll be able to glean some amazing insight into your shadow self and create compassion for individuals you'd previously felt very separate from.

Freely write about the times in your life you've exhibited the behaviors you dislike in these people. The deeper you can go here, the better. Ultimately, this practice will facilitate the development of a unity consciousness within you, helping you to bring peace to frustrating relationships and giving you a more forgiving perspective through which to see the world.

This practice has the potential to make visible the invisible parts of yourself that keep you from true happiness and inner peace.

By the end of this exercise, if you haven't been able to recognize yourself in these traits, your ego is standing in the way. Take some time to yourself to soften, become vulnerable, and stop hiding from your deepest truths. Because the more vulnerable you're willing to get with yourself during this exercise, the more your ego will be humbled and the more you will soften your judgments against others and yourself. And as the ego is checked and humbled, your perspective will shift from lack, fear, and dislike to acceptance, forgiveness, and patience—qualities essential to producing healthy, happy relationships—and a healthy, happy life.

In order to remove blockages to love and have a successful romantic relationship, you absolutely must be self-aware—you *must* be able to use others as mirrors for your innermost self so you do not remain trapped in a duality mentality and continue to view the world as "us versus them." And you must be able to look at another, see what bothers you, and realize it is merely a reflection of the way you see yourself at some deep, invisible level.

On the same note, you also must be able to look at another, see what you adore, and realize that you are witnessing a reflection of how amazing you are.

You are a human being with countless dimensions, and when you use the world around you as a mirror, you'll be able to gain insight into why you do what you do, and you'll have the awareness to shift your reality to what you truly desire.

Our relationships and lives are reflections of our many facets. And it's up to us to take action on the lessons those reflections provide.

By seeing yourself in others, you naturally reduce the degree to which you harshly judge yourself and others. Judgments transform into observations, and your perspective softens into compassion.

Exercise #2

To take this practice one step further and into the specific realm of romantic relationships, pull out your completed "Ideal Partner" worksheet. Next to the first question, "How are they with you?" write the statement, "How I am with them." Next to the second question, "How are they with others?" write the statement, "How I am with others." Next to the third question, "How are they with themselves?" write, "How I am with myself."

Just as others are mirrors for our inner selves, we are a mirror for others. So in order to call in your ideal partner, you must embody the aspects you seek. Adopt these ways of being in the world to attract your ideal partner.

Take a minute to review how you need to be with your current or future partner, yourself, and others in order to call in your ideal mate. To take this one step further, write affirmations on notecards and place them around your house, car, workspace, bathroom mirror, etc. Litter your house with loving reminders of who and how you must be to attract an ideal equal into your life.

Practice #2

At this point we've already done a lot of deep work, and I'm sure if you've gained anything so far, you feel at least some gratitude for these exercises. We want to cultivate that gratitude—that perspective of appreciation. In order to have more of what we love, we must love more of what we have. The more we amplify the gratitude we feel for the little, everyday things, the more we invite new things to be grateful for into our lives.

So, I'm going to challenge you to adopt another practice with a six-month time-frame. If you commit to this practice, your perspective of joy and peace will expand—and love, success, and anything else you are regularly focusing your attention on will abound. Keep in mind that energy flows where attention goes, which can add or detract from your existence. We'll go deeper into how to manage your attention later on.

Now it's time to stretch your habits and embrace a gratitude practice that will cradle your day in appreciation:

- Every night before you fall asleep, express your gratitude for a minimum of five things in your life. But instead of just bringing to mind five things to be grateful for, humble yourself to the life experience that's brought you these five things.

Feel the gratitude for these things in your mind and heart, don't just *think* about them and check them off some mental list.

- Every morning before you set one foot out of bed, bring to mind and heart five more things you're grateful for. Some can be the same as the night before, but some can be inspired by your dreams, your peaceful home, your good night's rest, or whatever else inspires you. Again, express this gratitude as a mental "thank you" to whatever force you desire—be it a personal force within you, an external/internal spiritual force, or simply nature's life force.

- Every morning as each foot touches the ground when you get out of bed, let the first foot be "thank" and the second foot be "you." Let your feet touching the ground represent an ultimate "thank you" for another day on Earth—another day in your body to experience life from your personal perspective.

By surrounding your day with gratitude, you energetically swaddle it like a cozy newborn, creating peace, safety, and appreciation for your amazing life.

When you see yourself in others, you expand your unity consciousness, which allows for deeper compassion, empathy, and love. And by adopting the behaviors you seek in a partner, you open your life to attracting your ideal mate. Top these exercises off with a twice-daily gratitude practice and boom! Your perspective shifts to witness the true love that surrounds your life—the love that is not temporary, but guides your deepest desires and highest dreams. View life from the eyes of love and you can and *will* call in such love.

Recognizing others as mirrors for your inner self and bringing consciousness to your life is imperative for creating a successful romantic relationship. But it's not the whole enchilada. Because in order to really make the transition into healthy relationships, you must clear your past relationships—drop the old, heavy, bloated "baggage" in the dumpster and buy yourself a hot, new, tiny purse—one that doesn't have the capacity to hold unhealthy relationship habits.

In the following chapter, you'll discover powerful boundary practices around what to do when you receive unwanted sexual attention and how to finally experience closure—with or without the participation of others—so you can move forward in life and love.

STEP 3
Clear the Past:
Close Doors to Open More

In order to become the person you want to be, you need to let go of the person you once were. As we attach to relationships and other people, so we attach to our self-images—to the roles we prescribe to ourselves over our lifetimes. Imagine going to a high-school reunion, or visiting your hometown and seeing someone from your past. How easy is it to stick someone in the same role from a decade or more past? We all want to be seen for who we are in the present moment rather than who we were many years ago, yet when we're faced with situations that inject us into those old roles, it can be too easy to accidentally fall right back into who we were rather than stand tall in who we are now, or better yet, be the best version of ourselves in each moment.

If we do not clear the past, we will continue to fall back into the past. If we do not close the doors to old relationships and self-images, we won't have the ability to open—or sometimes even to see—the new doors and opportunities available to us, as our energy will be diverted to maintaining a self that no longer serves our highest values.

In order to clear the past, you must first begin setting clear boundaries—keeping certain things out and other things in to step more fully into your authenticity and feel safer in your vulnerability. Second, you need to create closure in your life and with the past by closing energetic leaks from things left undone. Finally, you must feel true forgiveness for all past and current relationships—and this is not limited to romantic ones. True forgiveness is simultaneously expressed and felt for the self and for the other person. It bypasses reason or justification and moves straight into psychic healing.

In this chapter, you will learn how to build up to setting clearer and clearer boundaries, using your intuition and these lessons as a guide for action. You'll also learn how to safely express your emotions and access deep self-forgiveness to gain closure, with or without the participation of anyone else.

❦

Boundaries can be emotional, physical, mental, or spiritual. They can be financial, territorial, or relational.

Just as external boundaries lie between parcels of land, acting as borders, internal boundaries lie between what makes us feel safe and what makes us feel unsafe. The purpose of an internal boundary is to define a perimeter of comfort—to have a space that keeps certain things in and certain things out. It is important to assert boundaries when faced with situations that make you feel uncomfortable. These could be situations at work, with friends, with romantic relationships, or with sex . . . or a variety of other situations.

We each have different levels of comfort, and there is no right or wrong—no judgment—when it comes to other people's boundaries. So for those of you who do not struggle with unwanted sexual attention or feel this next section offers you nothing at all, imagine yourself in a situation that does instigate feelings of disempowerment—of threat to your physical, emotional, mental, or spiritual safety.

My last note before we dive in is that I do not want to limit this next topic to females, as I'm sure men have had their fair share of being sexualized or objectified by interested parties. But as a woman with female friends and female clients, I can speak from experience when I say that most women have experienced some form of unwanted sexual attention at some point in their lives, and too many women have a hard time speaking against such attention at the exact moment when they desire to do so.

Boundaries are particularly important in situations when you want to say "no" with all parts of your being, but you have been trained to be polite or are too ashamed to get that one-syllable word out of your mouth. And being an authentic, uninhibited, free individual without unconsciously leaking your sexual energy onto those you are not trying to attract sexually can be a precarious dance.

Learning how to let the giddy inner child run free while feeling safe in a non-sexual (but perhaps sensual) environment is a skill that can be learned by anyone willing to face discomfort.

So let's talk about discomfort for a moment, shall we?

How uncomfortable does it make you to be in a moment of disempowerment, such as that created by unwanted sexual attention? Do you feel funny about meeting the other person's eyes? Do you hide in a giggle, nervously trying to protect the other person's feelings? Do your social manners take over? Instead of letting this person feel shame, do you take it on because, after all, you don't want to hurt anyone or make them feel rejected?

Recall a time when you felt this way, if ever. Identify that level of discomfort and recognize that while those feelings are born in that moment, they carry through beyond that encounter and affect your deeper relationship with yourself. The areas most affected by disempowerment via unwanted sexual attention are:

1. Your feelings of self-worth: Your subconscious may believe your physical body is all you have to offer—all you are good for;

2. Your feelings of self-trust: Your subconscious might begin to feel you cannot trust yourself to stand up for yourself, which feeds feelings of unworthiness; and

3. Your future relationships: You may begin to feel cynical about men (or women), wondering if they're all the same, or at least incredulous that so many of them are oblivious or careless about how they're making you feel; this can lead to feeling unsafe with intimacy.

Fortunately, there is a way to bypass that particular type of discomfort by getting uncomfortable in a *different* way. But don't let that intimidate you, because if you're willing to get uncomfortable on your own terms, you will actually begin to reverse the effects of past disempowering situations of unwanted sexual attention.

Are you willing to get uncomfortable on your own terms?

If yes, then read on, because you're about to receive a tool that, if used, will change the way you relate to receiving unwanted sexual attention *forever*.

Exercise #3

Please note:

- In the beginner phase of using this tool, you will likely use it after the event has occurred.

- In the intermediate phase of using this tool, you will use it during the event.

- As an advanced user, you will apply the use of this tool before the event will occur, thereby bypassing the event altogether.

The tool: *Verbalizing the unspoken energies of the moment.*

For the beginner:

An uncomfortable, sexualized event occurs. You can recognize that it was uncomfortable because now that it's over, you feel slightly embarrassed or ashamed, and you keep thinking about what you wish you had done differently. The name of the person you were in this exchange with creeps you out, and you may feel dread thinking about seeing this person anytime soon.

It is time to verbalize the unspoken energies of the moment and liberate yourself from feelings of discomfort and shame.

The goal of this exercise is to feel complete with the energetic exchange. Before the conversation, there is a huge gap where your mind can come in and harass you for not doing something better or behaving in a different way. This is your opportunity to close that gap, right the wrong, put all cards on the table, and clear the energy. The ultimate goal is to create a safe space within yourself and this experience, and also to clear the air so that if you run into the person again in public, there is no awkwardness.

Here is what to do:

1. Contact the person and ask them to be in touch via phone when they have some time and space to have a conversation (the phone is important so that you can be in your own, strong energy field when you speak with them);

   Text or email: Hi, Chris. I'd like to set up a time to have a phone convo with you soon. When is good for you?

2. When you get on the phone with them, confirm they are in a space where they can talk;

   "Hi, Chris. It's Emily. I just want to confirm you're in a space where we can chat for a few. Is now still a good time?"

3. Once confirmed, tell them you felt uncomfortable about your last encounter. Tell them exactly how their behavior made you feel uncomfortable;

   "Thanks for being willing to hop on the phone with me. I just need to let you know that the last time we were together I felt uncomfortable about where our conversation (or encounter) went. I felt unable to express my discomfort at the time, but when you said _____, it resonated back to other times in my life I've received unwanted sexual attention."

4. Take responsibility for not speaking up sooner, and affirm that this conversation is not to blame them or make them feel bad, but simply to *put a voice to the discomfort;*

   "I'm sure you didn't intend to make me feel uncomfortable, and I apologize for not speaking up at the moment. I'm learning how to speak up for myself, and this is a perfect example of how I can do better next time. But for now, I just want you to know that I'm not trying to make you feel bad, I'm just putting a voice to a situation I felt very uncomfortable about."

5. Listen as they speak. Pause before responding. Inquire within to see if what they're saying needs a response for you to feel complete with this process.

   a) If not, then close the conversation.

   b) If what they are saying does require you to communicate further, continue to take responsibility for not bringing this up sooner and do not get defensive, blame, or shame. On the other end of the spectrum, do not allow them to make you feel bad for their actions—do not take on blame or shame. Simply state the facts and get off the phone.

   "Again, thank you for hopping on the phone with me and allowing me to further my spiritual journey by having this conversation."

When you hang up, you might feel unsettled. You might feel a lump in your throat or a knot in your gut. This expressive action can be uncomfortable. Just remember that the goal of this is to move the energy of the past while practicing standing up for yourself in the present. This exercise builds self-trust so that the next time you encounter unwanted sexual attention, you can perhaps practice from the intermediate phase.

When *not* to use this tactic:

- If you're knowingly dealing with a mentally unstable individual, or
- If you're knowingly dealing with someone not mature enough to hear your concerns (someone who will try to blame you and make you feel bad).

The above are judgment calls you must make to keep yourself safe. Go with your gut over your head.

For the intermediate user:

In the midst of receiving unwanted sexual attention, don't disregard it or try to talk yourself out of what you are sensing at a deeper level. Once you give someone's come-on validity and you feel uncomfortable in their presence, then depending on how far things have gone, you can either use this communication tool or go a whole different route:

1. Use the tool and verbalize your discomfort

   a) If this is happening with someone you know pretty well, or will see again in casual or professional settings, then speak out.

   b) Tell this person that you're uncomfortable with what they're saying, the energetic exchange that's taking place, the topic of conversation, or whatever else might be going on in this moment.

   c) Say this without a smile and without giggling. Keep your spine straight, your shoulders back, your head upright, and look them square in the eyes. If you weren't in this position before, assume it at this moment. The power of this nonverbal communication will speak more loudly than your words, and it will cut off any future unwanted form of attention from this person.

2. Walk away

   a) Seriously, straight up, walk away. You don't have to do anything else. You don't have to be polite. You don't have to explain yourself. The ONE thing you have to do is show yourself enough respect to remove yourself from an undesirable situation. Trust yourself to have your own back, and then have it.

   b) Imagine if a friend knew how uncomfortable you were. They'd lash out at the person, or grab your arm and take you away. Be your own bestie and bail.

For the advanced user:

As you hone the skill of verbalizing the unspoken energies of the moment and feel more empowered to speak up against unwanted sexual attention, you'll trust your instincts more and more. You'll learn that when you feel weird, it's because the person you're around is sexualizing the moment and it's making you feel uncomfortable.

Immediately when you notice the person's energy shift (and consequently *your* energy shift) you can nip this whole dance in the bud.

Here's what to do:

1. Immediately verbalize the unspoken energies of the moment— put words to the energetic shift. Be prepared that *they might not even be aware* that their energy has shifted. They might only just be starting to feel sexual. That's okay, because you've honed your intuition so you're going to be able to sense the shift sooner than they will. They may even deny the shift, so this is when it's super important to trust your instinct and be prepared to be okay looking a little self-involved.

2. By voicing the energetic shift right in the moment it occurs, you can easily bow out of the conversation, or you can redirect the focus of the conversation, or the other person might just choose to leave. If you're talking to a more enlightened being, they'll love your self-awareness, and a new, awesome conversation might ensue.

By learning how to verbalize the unspoken energies of the moment and applying this skill in your life, you no longer need to withhold your innocent, childlike, playful energy. That creative, intuitive, receptive feminine frequency can be honored in its fullest form, because you create safety in your inner being by knowing that you can and *will* take care of yourself first and foremost.

Also know that it's okay to feel uncomfortable with only *some* people. It's okay to act flirty and love attention from 80% of people, but feel uncomfortable flirting or receiving sexual attention from the other 20%. This tool gives you the skills to start and stop your unconscious leaky sexual energy that's flowing onto *everyone* and calling in that unwanted 20%. Once you practice this and become an advanced user of verbalizing the unspoken energies of the moment, you'll be able to feel safe in your fully free, sexualized self around everyone.

Setting boundaries keeps you feeling safe and empowered to be your authentic you. Whether you're setting a boundary around how many hours per week you're willing to work or what sacrifices you are and are not willing to make for your romantic relationship, defining and verbalizing boundaries is an important practice to build self-trust.

In the above scenario of creating and asserting boundaries around unwanted sexual attention, you are inviting in an opportunity to heal your past. If ever you've felt uncomfortable in a sexual situation, by setting boundaries and speaking them outright *now*, you're re-establishing the relationship you have with yourself around this sensitive topic.

You actually heal what happened in the past by standing against it happening again in the present. In doing so, you're clearing your past, and you're closing the door to the part of yourself that allowed others to take advantage of you. This is one way to create closure around past injustices.

Another way to create closure is to come full circle with an energetic exchange.

An energetic exchange can be as simple as having taken a loan from someone you felt uncomfortable receiving money from; paying them back is the solution. Once you do that, you no longer have that tiny weight on your shoulders that just sat there, possibly for many years, unobserved and largely unnoticed. Imagine having many of those tiny little weights. Carrying lots of open energetic loops will inevitably become a heavy burden.

An energetic exchange can also be complex: for instance, a long-term relationship that ends abruptly and without deep understanding or communication around where the rift began, what evoked it, and how you could do better next time. It leaves you feeling unsure and provoked every time you consider the relationship, and the regret, confusion, pain, and distrust carries over into future relationships. In this case, one of the following solutions will help you to create closure and move your love life forward.

For a moment, visualize this term "energetic exchange" as a circle. A completed energetic exchange will be a nice, whole circle. But without completing an energetic exchange, you have a gap in the circle. This is where so many of us lose energy—broken circles. It is so *important* to close that loop—to come full-circle—so that you stop losing energy on past events.

Fortunately, even in the case of the incomplete relationship, you do not need the involvement of another person to close an energetic circle.

There are many ways to close your energetic circle, but I prefer these two methods:

1. Write a letter you do not intend to send
2. Practice Ho'oponopono

For the following exercises, bring to mind one person you have history with that feels unsettled. Trust your intuition and go with the first person that comes to mind. Thinking about this person should evoke a feeling deep inside your gut. You'll practice both exercises with the same person in order to fully release the past and heal the relationship.

Worksheet #3

Write a letter you do not intend to send. By taking the time to sit down and handwrite a letter that *you will not send*, you give yourself permission to say all that was not said—to express without holding back, and to really let everything flow easily and fully. Even though you are writing, not speaking, this process clears your throat's energy center. By letting out all the things you did not say onto this piece of paper, you liberate yourself from choking back your true feelings surrounding the particular energetic exchange you're working with. To assist in releasing this energy, allow yourself to make guttural noises while writing or emoting.

As you hold this person in mind, identify the most potent emotion you're consciously in touch with. Now it's time to write a letter you do not intend to send.

In the workbook, you will find Worksheet #3, entitled "The Letter." Go ahead and fill it out, and begin to close one of your energetic loops.

Once you've written this letter, move on to the next exercise.

Practice #3

Practice Ho'oponopono. Ho'oponopono is an ancient Hawaiian forgiveness practice, and its effects are profound. The prayer operates on the belief that we are 100% responsible for our realities and that by forgiving ourselves for the actions of another, we clear their consciousness of the same act. I encourage you to read more about Ho'oponopono if you are interested, but what is more important than understanding it is applying it within your life. Therefore, I have given you access to my twenty minute Ho'oponopono guided meditation with your purchase of this book. Go to *www.emilyrosecoaching.com/byblh-meditation* to download your complimentary guided meditation now!

Create the time and space to free yourself from past traumas, clear the past, and experience energetic closure in your life and relationships. Go ahead and get comfortable, bring the person to mind you've chosen for these two exercises, and go through the guided forgiveness meditation with me.

By choosing to forgive the person who has hurt you, you set yourself free of the karmic wound caused by the pain of the event. Ease your heart now, and forgive with this powerful prayer.

Feeling true forgiveness for your partners in all past and current relationships is a form of psychic healing, and coupled with the practice of writing out your deepest feelings, it will reset the way you feel about past circumstances, relationships, and people. It will help you to complete your circle—to close your energetic loop and close the doors to the past, so that you may open your heart to a new future that is more in alignment with your highest desires. And when you practice setting clear boundaries in *any* life circumstance that threatens your feelings of safety, self-respect, or empowerment, you are sending the message to the Universe that you're ready to walk a path filled with self-trust and self-love.

In doing so, you're empowering yourself to step more fully into your authenticity and feel safer in your vulnerability, which allows you to call in more authentic romantic relationships and experience a deeper emotional connection during intimacy.

Using your intuition as a guide to set boundaries, to safely express your emotions, and to access self-forgiveness will free you from your past and open you to your future. But to make sure you cease repeating the same patterns, you must also have a psychological understanding of the relationship dynamics you just might be playing out. In the next chapter, you will learn the most common relationship dynamic; once you are aware of it, it will change the whole game. You'll also learn how to examine your past relationships to glean insight into unconscious patterns and then use that information to create your ideal future relationships. Finally, you'll learn the single most obstructive thing that blocks love from entering your life.

STEP 4
Receive Love: Understand the Pattern and Break the Habits

Love is something we not only want, but need as human beings. Yet taking the time to actually *receive* love from another is infrequently practiced. In order to have a balanced relationship with giving and receiving of any kind—including love—you first need to understand the psychology of why you've been engaging with relationships the way you have. There's a formula, and once you know it, engagement becomes a choice, not a habit. You also need to know how to learn from past relationships in order to build your ideal future relationship and call in your dream partner.

This chapter will show you the quickest path to freeing yourself from the love habits that have kept you in heart-breaking relationships, along with the *easiest* way to open your heart and begin feeling *real love* as soon as possible.

If I've learned one thing from the many (many) relationships I've been through, it's that each one serves a purpose—each one teaches a lesson. And perhaps more relevant, you're never really single if you relationship hop.

Jumping from one relationship to the next without giving yourself time in between to shift your energy out of the relationship you just came from invites your new relationship to have the same problems as the old one. This also applies to the people who *do* give themselves a lot of time in between relationships, but still do not go into the grief and explore the lessons from each past relationship before entering into the next one.

As easy as this concept is to understand—that you should not get into a new relationship without fully processing your past one—I bet you're interested in where the urge to be in a relationship comes from. Or better still, why you're continually attracted to relationships that don't work out. Why have you had so many heartbreaks, or why have you broken so many dang hearts? Why are you attracted to the people who don't give you the time of day and repelled by the people who are ready to dote on you and make you the center of their Universe?

Read on to find out how my path led me to a deeper understanding of these confounding relationship dynamics.

As you can probably guess, I'm not about to tell you it's wrong to have many relationships. But I do want to share with you the limitations unconscious relationship hopping can have on one's personal growth and development.

When I relationship hopped, I used to call it "taste-testing."

Of course I did not taste everyone—ew. But I did view the delectable assortment of men in the world as mysterious mini-Universes still unknown to me, with infinite potential to be "the one."

So it was my charge to sample the selections, quickly determine if each was indeed my knight in shining armor, and then either fall momentarily in love, or demolish the budding relationship near its inception.

Needless to say, this game offered a rush of love-chemicals—a ride so addicting, I happily fooled myself and others into thinking each valid candidate was "different," and therefore worth diving deep into relationship with.

Much later in my relationship-hopping life, I came to discover the two predominant roles in most romantic relationships today: the role of the love-drug dealer, and the role of the love-drug addict.

Now don't fool yourself into thinking you know the intricacies of these two roles just by reading their titles. We're about to dive into the psychology of commitment here, and I wouldn't want you to miss out on one of the key factors that holds you back from having a successful romantic relationship.

Some people lean toward the role of the love-drug dealer, and some lean toward the role of the love-drug addict, while still others play alternating roles in different relationships. As you read on, you'll recognize which role you tend toward and which role you attract as your counterpart in romantic relationships. Remember, it does indeed take two to tango.

The Love-Drug Dealer

As the love-drug dealer, you are actively in control of the relationship. You may view the other person as uninteresting, unintelligent, or just not quite up to par. And since they're never quite what you're looking for, you seek to change them.

You determine what your time together looks like—what you do and when. You determine the depth of connection, because it's you who is always withholding. You tend to spend a lot of time away from the relationship and tend to be extremely private or keep secrets from your partner.

In this role, you're always on the verge of leaving them, and sometimes you do, only to return in a state of desperation, because—let's face it—the love that person offers you seems totally unconditional, and that alone feeds your need for the acceptance and love human beings crave.

The love-drug dealer simultaneously wants two opposing situations with every fiber of their being: to be single and fully free, and to be in their dream partnership with their one true love—their soul mate. This internal push and pull projects itself onto whatever relationships love-drug dealers find themselves in.

Have you been a pusher of that oh-so-scrumptious drug called love? If not, maybe you've found yourself on the other side of this dramatic dance . . .

The Love-Drug Addict

In an especially sneaky role, as the love-drug addict you truly believe you are 100% committed to your partner. You give and give and give. You love "unconditionally." Your love-drug dealer may ask you to change, to accommodate their needs. And so you do. Because you love them.

So why is this role sneaky?

You see, as the love-drug addict, you have tricked yourself into believing you are doing your best, giving all of your love, and truly trying your hardest in the relationship. And you very well may be. The problem is, you picked a partner who didn't want your love to begin with. So before the relationship even started, you selected a person who wouldn't be able to receive or reciprocate such undying affection.

The other problem is, you picked a person who craves the doting you offer, and because of this, until you've had enough and finally decide done is done, this relationship will persist. You will have to be the one to break it off. And you will, because when you've given more than you knew you had to give, you'll realize that you've given yourself. Since the love-drug dealer never really wanted you to begin with, you've never felt comfortable being your true self with this person. Ultimately, you've sacrificed yourself for them. Humans are not meant to be less than who they truly are, so this relationship dynamic is unsustainable.

The love-drug addict selects unavailable or inappropriate partners from the inception of the relationship. In fact, that's the only type of person they're attracted to. Because it is this type of unavailable partner that they can pour love into and walk away from guilt-free, knowing they gave the relationship their all.

What defines an unavailable or inappropriate partner, you ask?

The most obvious are large age differences, long distance relationships, married people, or people who, from the get-go, very clearly express their desire for nothing too serious.

Something to keep in mind is that people can play different roles in different relationships. I know I've played both many times throughout the years. And it's possible to actually flip roles throughout a single relationship. A love-drug dealer may plant the seeds of being a love-drug addict—doting on their new partner while they fall in love. But if you know what to look for, you'll see that this person's unavailability will eventually push them into the love-drug dealer role and you into the love-drug addict role.

Now why do people play these games?

It would seem this kind of drama and pain isn't worth the love-chemical rush one receives in the beginning of such a dance.

The bottom line is that most people involved in love-drug relationships are uncomfortable with solitude. They fear being alone because they are scared to get to know themselves.

Relationships grown from this fear of being alone are inevitably unfulfilling, because no one can truly love you until you learn to love yourself.

In the end, love-drug relationships combust due to emotional exhaustion and a desperate desire for authentic partnership.

Which brings me to my next points:

- This dynamic does not apply to ALL relationships—thank God.
- A healthy relationship is balanced in love, input, and energy.
- A healthy relationship involves communication from a place of inner clarity.

- A healthy relationship involves complete authenticity from both people in the relationship.
- And you can have a healthy relationship with large age differences or long distances, depending on your level of commitment after you've identified this dynamic and healed the beliefs that had you engaging from a love-drug level.

In 2007, I had my last of what I consider to be unhealthy relationships.

I was on the love-drug addict side of things and I went through an especially brutal heartbreak. After a few hours of wailing, I was determined to never feel that way again.

From that moment on, I began to educate myself about relationships. In doing so, I sought therapy, cleared blockages, realigned my desires, and eventually stopped activating my love-chemical addiction.

For years, it was in the rare single-state that I found my most valuable lessons on relationships. Because it was in this state I was able to tap into my authentic self and be fully *me*.

From this space I stepped outside the relationship dance, and from there it was relatively easy to see beyond the narrow scope of one-on-one relating and witness the patterns keeping me from being my best self.

Perhaps more importantly, it became more apparent that how I was with myself determined how others were with me.

Being single gave me the time to build a respectful, loving relationship with myself first.

To top it off, getting out of the game gave me the space and time to stop carrying past hurts and projecting old wounds onto whatever relationship came next.

I was able to start clean: to learn, digest, and assimilate lessons from past relationships before embarking on something new.

Looking back at that transition, I remember my biggest fear about letting go of the emotional rollercoaster ride that so excited my internal and external senses was that I'd never again feel such extreme, passionate love.

I was afraid that if I didn't engage in a game with love—with that oh-so-addictive push-pull aspect egging me along—it would be a wholly dull experience, void of emotional highs. I had to ask myself if I was willing to sacrifice the highs to get rid of the lows. And I was.

Now, having experienced a healthy relationship I defined as a "dream come true" romance, I can tell you that when love is rooted in love rather than fear, it is so much deeper, truer, and more fulfilling than any chemical-driven game can ever be. Every day is a high. My median emotional bar has been raised, and life is simply amazing.

The sooner you stop relationship hopping and instead tune into what those relationships are seeking to fulfill within your psyche, the sooner you'll be able to get clear on who you are and what you really want in your life.

It may be monogamy; it may not.

Either way, your newfound clarity and authenticity will attract your deepest desires, and in turn, deliver your dream-come-true relationship.

You don't need to continue to chase your dream. You can live it. Now.

How?

Practice #4

Simply put, you will need to adopt a mantra. While this method is most useful when you're single and first meeting someone of interest, rather than when you're immersed in a love-drug relationship, it's still possible to shift such a relationship's dynamic, albeit very difficult. Either way, if you've identified with one of these love-drug roles and want to break free of this destructive cycle, your new mantra is:

"I let him show me who he is. I let him show me who he is. I let him show me who he is."

Of course, your new mantra might have a different pronoun:

"I let her show me who she is. I let her show me who she is. I let her show me who she is."

Repeat this phrase over and over in your brain when you notice your thoughts leap into future fantasy-mode. It will keep you grounded in the moment with this new person and allow you to see them for all they're offering.

While swooning for a new beau, it's all too easy dismiss quirks and deem them "adorable." Yet those quirks are insights into how compatible you may or may not be long-term. If you notice those quirks so clearly in those first moments, even if you dismiss them as endearing, that's a big red flag for what might grate on your nerves once the rose-colored lenses fade away.

This is not to say that your ideal mate won't have quirks or that they won't do things that grate on your nerves. It is to say that your ideal mate's quirks will be minute compared to the plethora of awesomeness they bring to your life. In addition, if you've got your new mantra running through your head when you meet your ideal mate, you might still notice the quirks, but you'll be able to more consciously weigh their impact rather than making excuses for them or denying them altogether. You'll have the wherewithal to see both the quirk and the person sitting in front of you for all that they are—or at least who they're showing you they are—in that moment. You'll be less inclined to be swept off your feet, and you'll be able to keep your head on your shoulders while you practically evaluate this candidate for companionship. In the bonus section of the book, you'll find a guide on hopeless romanticism versus practical romanticism which instructs you in how to honor both the ideal and the practical in your romantic relationship.

For now, suffice it to say that only once you've deemed this new prospect as a potentially good fit for partnership—similar interests, great sense of humor, intelligent, awesome chemistry, etc.—should you move on to planning another experience together, you will continue your mantra throughout the entire date.

We all know it takes a great while to get to know a person (if we ever really do), and while you're stewing in the steamy romance of the first few months of dating, you'll want to refrain as much as possible from shoving their character in a box.

"Oh, so he's a Mac guy. That means he must be this, this, and this."

"Oh, she used the word 'Universe.' That means she must believe exactly what I do."

No.

Bad.

Cease those assumptions and let this person show you who they are.

And let them *keep* showing you.

When you listen, don't be categorizing them or thinking of the next thing you can say. Leave your mind open, and actually *hear* what they're saying. And repeat to yourself over and over, "I let him show me who he is." "I let her show me who she is." This practice can be the single most effective tool in helping you to identify your unwanted relationship patterns and to break your bad love habits *before* you're in the midst of a tumultuous relationship.

At this point, I'm sure your brain is reviewing your past relationships and seeing all the ways in which this love-drug dynamic influenced your and your ex's attitudes and actions, and ultimately shaped the outcome of the relationship.

It can be easy to remember the pain associated with an ex, but to learn the full lesson, it's also important to see the value that came out of being in the relationship.

Worksheet #4

In the workbook, you'll find a series of worksheets entitled "Examining the Exes." Go ahead and grab those worksheets and use them to specify the lessons you've learned from your past relationships and just how these past relationships have been preparing you for your ideal partner.

> To start this process off, bring to mind three of your most influential relationships. These will be the relationships that taught you the most lessons and impacted your life and heart the most deeply. Write down the names of your exes from these relationships on the first worksheet. Under each name, list the ways in which these relationships have been preparing you for your ideal partner.
>
> For example, one of your exes might have shouted and screamed like an overgrown child. From that, you might learn that your ideal partner will be level-headed and non-violent.
>
> Or perhaps one of your exes used to get you flowers and write you love notes every so often, and you loved it!

You'd definitely note that your ideal mate will express their love in a similar fashion.

On the next page of the worksheet, identify the commonalities between these exes and their behaviors that taught you so much. Do you see a theme? The information that comes up here is for your personal reflection. When you've finished finding the similarities between the lists on the first page, see if you can dig deeper into the lessons you've learned from these relationships. For example, if you were to examine the screamer, you might find that this person taught you that you feel belittled when you're yelled at, and now as a full-fledged adult, you do not need to be subjected to such belittlement. Maybe it resonated back to childhood and revealed an open wound. Maybe the yelling made you feel disempowered. But now, from this perspective, you're actually *empowered* by the event because you know you will no longer stand for such nonsense in your world. Or if we look at the ex who brought you flowers and wrote love notes, maybe you learned that one of your love languages is receiving gifts, and now you know why you love to give gifts so much.

Once you've completed this section, move on to defining your dream partner. It's important for you to really specify the experience of the person you want to call in. At the beginning of this book, we used a similar worksheet to figure out *how* that person is in the world so that you could realize how you need to be in order to attract them. Now it's time to define your *experience* of this person, so you will be able to know when you meet someone whether they fit with your ideal desires. And if you happen to be in a relationship while reading this book, still fill this section out. It will offer insight into whether or not your current partner is your ultimate match.

Note: Keep in mind that again, your ideal mate will have quirks and traits you cannot even fathom, and some of these may bother you. But ultimately, the big, important factors will align.

If your spiritual, physical, mental, and emotional needs are met, then quirks and bothers won't keep you from being with your partner.

Finally, use the last page of the worksheet set to freewrite about your experience of your ideal mate. Get wild here. Have fun. Dream big.

The final and super important factor that will help you to have a successful romantic relationship is so basic it's crazy:

You need to be able to receive love.

Think about the last time you said, "I love you." Think about how often you say it! To friends, to family, and to romantic partners.

Now think about the last time you said, "I receive your love." Eh? Ever? Maybe not.

Exercise #4

It is so easy to give love. We give it all day long in so many forms. But to simply receive love when someone else tells us they love us is unbelievably powerful. The next time someone says they love you, take a moment and soak it in before tossing the reciprocation back their way. If they're a close enough peep, tell them what you're doing, and go ahead and close your eyes and receive that love. If you're with a romantic partner, use your words; look them in the eyes and say, "I receive your love" while focusing on the feeling of receiving.

This simple yet powerful practice will open your heart and shift your relationship to relationships. You'll go from giving until you're blue in the face to finding a place of balance in your giving/receiving nature.

To have a successful romantic relationship, you must be able to both give *and* receive love. You must also know what you can and cannot compromise in a romantic relationship, which the lessons from this chapter will help you to determine.

By looking to the past and examining those educational exes, you can take your lessons into future relationships and call in a partner who is more in alignment with your needs and desires. And when you release the addiction to the love-drug chemical rush that happens at the onset of entering an inevitably difficult relationship, you free yourself to attract the healthiest of relationships with the potential for long-term commitment—if you so desire.

The final chapter of this book contains the cherry on top: three incredible tools that will help you to consciously manifest whatever it is you desire in any and every area of your life—including romantic relationships. It will teach you how to reprogram the voice in your head to be your new BFF, how to make affirmations actually work, and how to love your body more deeply and unconditionally than you ever have before.

STEP 5
Manifest Consciously: Attract Your Dream Relationship NOW

Congratulations! You've done so much great work. In this last step, you're going to learn how to attract your dream relationship by taking an active yet balanced role in co-creating your reality with the Universe. This does not mean blindly affirming your way into manifestation (as many popular practices suggest), but instead consciously co-creating from an educated and experience-based place. You'll also learn how to use your mind as the tool it is so that you can reprogram old thought patterns and belief systems to work for you and create your ideal present reality. Finally, you'll learn how to deepen your self-love, accept and appreciate your body for all that it is, and in turn open your life to more fulfilling intimate relationships.

This last step really is essential in transforming your relationship to romantic relationships and breaking your bad love habits. It will facilitate your ultimate shift in love and life, helping you to be your best self. Complete these final exercises and practices, and watch your love life—and your love for life—expand.

In order to not just break your bad love habits, but to instill *healthy* love habits and *call in* your dream-come-true relationship and life, you need to know how to properly use tools such as affirmations and positive thinking. It would seem that the New Age movement has covered it all; however, in this chapter you'll find a twist on affirmations you won't see anywhere else—and it's the twist that makes them *work*.

To put it simply, affirmations are only as good as your experience of what you're trying to call in.

Here's how that works: I'm sure you've figured out that trying to tell yourself you're going to win the lottery hasn't actually made you win the lottery. That's because you don't really believe it, because you've never experienced receiving a lot of money out of the blue.

Fortunately, you don't actually have to experience what you want to the degree that you want it; you just have to experience a *taste* of what you want so you know it can be true for you—*then* you can affirm it.

For example, when I lived in Maui I met a man who showed me that the full package actually existed. He was unbelievably gorgeous, totally zenned out, super present, completely wonderful, humble, powerful, masculine, tender, loving, considerate, all those amazing things and more. Plus he was gorgeous. Did I mention that already?

We became friends, and while it turned out we did not share a romantic connection, just knowing that a man like this was on Earth expanded my belief system, which made me able to call in my dream partner.

From that place of possibility, I *believed* that a dude who was the complete package actually existed out there—and because I experienced this firsthand, it made it possible for me to attract my complete-package partner into my life.

Exercise #5

The following steps will help you open your reality to the possibility of what you want to call in, whether that's more money, deeper friendships, or more conscious romantic relationships.

So let your affirmations work for you; use the following practices to call in what you truly desire.

- **Work toward what you want.**

  If you want a romantic relationship, don't sit idly by and repeat the same old relationship patterns and habits you've had for years. If you want a sudden stream of income, don't go home after work and watch TV all night. If you want more time with your family, don't say "yes" to unnecessary projects or people that detract from your fulfillment. Be proactive in life, stay open, and prepare for the best.

- **Let go.**

  This may seem like the exact opposite of what I just said, but it's not. After bringing to mind and heart what you desire, let it come in by releasing it from your thoughts. If you obsess over what you're wanting, you're not allowing it the space to arrive. So bring it to mind every so often, but don't hold your breath. Go on enjoying your life without it, striving to do your best, and working toward your goal, and the Universe will inevitably catch up.

- **Pay attention to coincidences.**

  We've all heard "everything happens for a reason." So let's give things a reason to happen! Honor coincidences, stay open to signs, and pay attention to your gut when it speaks. Sometimes our busy minds and busy days distract us from the inner self that whispers—if only we will listen. Paying attention to coincidences will help you tune in to the constant awesomeness that surrounds you . . . and call in more coincidences to boot.

- **Use your gratitude to practice honoring all the bits and pieces of what you're calling in.**

  Every morning and every night, notice specific things you are grateful for that reflect some aspect of what you're calling in.

By placing your attention on, let's say, this beautiful person's empathetic nature, or the unexpected refund you received today, you're emphasizing the value of those elements of your day. This alone will do wonders for attracting into your life the thing that you're affirming. (Refer back to the gratitude practices in Chapter Two to surround your day with gratitude.) Try using the nightly gratitude practice to emphasize the pieces of your day that reflect what you're calling in. Only affirm what you know to be true from experience, and call in what you can right now.

As you align yourself with your truest desires, the Universe *will* offer you experiences that activate your ability to manifest your dream-reality. Work toward your wants, and then *let them go to let them flow* into your life. Pay attention to your intuition and the magic of coincidences, and to the elements of your day that reflect what you're calling in.

These practices, when applied regularly, will help you open your life to receiving your deepest desires from an intuitive, centered, proactive, and—perhaps most importantly—*realistic* place.

Because only after you experience a hint of what you're looking to manifest will you be able to use affirmations to their fullest potential—and you'll finally see the effects you desire.

All the exercises, practices, meditations, and guidelines you've read in this book so far work toward shifting your mindset to the positive—toward helping you to see the abundance of joy and love in your life and to experience the worthiness you deserve to feel. However, there is one practice that, if incorporated with the rest of the journey presented here in this book, will totally change your life forever.

At the end of Chapter Two, I mentioned that you will attract anything you direct your attention to, since energy flows where attention goes. This can work for you or against you. So it is especially important for you to use the ultimate tool at your disposal to make sure you're calling in all the good stuff: your brain.

Your brain is a supercomputer. It is charged and ready to send you messages of encouragement or notices of resignation and defeat. The voice in your head constantly bombards you with thoughts, considerations, evaluations, and judgments—which is actually fantastic. This allows you to see the level your subconscious is operating at, and to shift it accordingly.

So far in this book, we've worked with reframing the deep belief systems which lie at the foundation of thoughts and emotions.

Now it's time to tackle this bad boy from the top down, which is one of the most effective ways of changing your reality for the better.

You'll notice that as your belief systems begin to reorient to the positive, your thoughts will naturally go there as well.

This exercise will give the process a super-boost and kick your conscious mind into the right gear.

Worksheet #5

In the workbook, you'll find Worksheet #5, entitled "Reprogramming." Just as you would with a computer, you're going to go into your mind and examine and replace the old programming with new programming. You're not going to get all fancy and creative here; it's just very basic 1100101 in mental coding.

In the left-hand column of the worksheet, write down fifteen negative thoughts you hear your mind telling you right now. If you're having trouble coming up with fifteen, get up and walk around. Go look in the mirror, then sit back down and record what you hear that you'd like to replace with kind words. If you still have blank spaces, throughout the next few days continue to list negative thoughts that come to mind.

Once you have your fifteen negative thoughts written down, in the right-hand column write *the exact opposite* of each thought, formulated in a positive phrase.

For example, if your mind said, "I'm depressed," you'd write "I'm happy," rather than "I'm not depressed." Another example: across from "I am not satisfied with my lifestyle," you'd reprogram that thought with, "I am satisfied with my lifestyle," instead of "I love my lifestyle!" Eventually you'll want to exclaim your love for your lifestyle, but right now we're just going in and changing a thought pattern to the positive. By starting at square one, you can easily identify and replace thoughts without having to remember what you were supposed to replace a certain thought with.

If you want to extend this practice further, go beyond fifteen naysaying judgments and take a few days to write down the whole array of negative thoughts that come through. Continue to write what you hear your mind say that isn't so nice, and then write the positive replacement for that thought shortly thereafter.

Reprogramming the mind differs from creating affirmations in just the slightest way. When you come up with affirmations based on your experience of things you want more of—love, money, success, inner peace—you are using your mind to dream up something you want in the future, and then you're using your present moment or past memories to create a foundation for this new affirmation.

When you reprogram your mind, you're not trying to dream up something for the future—in fact, you're not trying to dream up anything at all. The purpose is not to attract something new into your life; it is simply to change your mindset, and to do so in the present. Instead of using past memories or future desires to shape your new mental programming, you're using your thoughts at the present moment to create new thoughts the second they occur.

The outcome from successful reprogramming is a positive mental attitude.

Use both tools to increase the joy and love in your life—to manifest consciously and create your ideal relationship. But remember that when you want to receive more love in your life, feel more confident and self-assured, and have successful, intimate, romantic relationships, it is imperative you feel worthy of the aforementioned things.

Reprogramming your mind, doing your shadow work, going on a positivity diet, creating gratitude practices, forgiving the past, and being the type of person you want to attract are amazing ways of helping yourself to feel such self-worth. But I am going to offer you one more practice that will be the kicker for shifting your relationship with yourself.

The following practice teaches you how to love your physical body.

With perfectionists' eyes, we stare at our bodies and shame the vessels that hold our life force. This dysfunctional relationship damages our ability to receive love, which hinders our ability to freely give love, as well. The warped view that we have of our physical bodies reflects the warped view we have of our innermost selves. In other words, when we feel ugly on the outside, we feel ugly on the inside.

Practice #5

The body love practice: for the next seven consecutive days, take twenty minutes in the morning before getting out of bed (ideally), or in the evening before falling asleep, and—tiny patch by tiny patch— touch your body gently with both hands and tell it you love it. Start with your toes, which alone should take at least two minutes. Hold them in your hands, squeeze them, touch them lightly, all the while intentionally sending them love through your hands and verbally saying, "I love you, toes." If you can, say this out loud.

You're also welcome to dote on them more and appreciate them for all they do for you. "Toes, you hold me upright and I'm so grateful you're there to keep me balanced.

I love the way you feel when tickled or sunken into the sand. Look at that little freckle right there! How cute you are, little freckle." Yes. Take the time to sound like an insane person, and don't be ashamed. Have fun with it!

Bit by bit, move up your body. So the next place you go? The tops and bottom of your feet, of course. Maybe your heel. "Oh feet, how awesome you are. I love you so much, feet. You carry the weight of my whole body—and you're cute, too! I love you, feet. Thank you so much for all that you do for me." You get the idea.

For seven days straight, take twenty minutes (minimum) to love your body—to give your body love. This is a profound practice that will help you to shift not just your mental attitude concerning your body, but your emotional attitude as well. You'll *feel* the love for your body, and you'll realize how special it truly is, for there is not another body like yours in the world. It is *your* body holding *your* spirit, and it deserves your love and appreciation.

When you deepen your self-love and learn to accept and appreciate your body for all that it is, you open your life to more fulfilling intimate relationships. You also naturally begin to shift your mental programming. Of course, befriending the voice in your head is also a necessary and powerful step, one which will help you to shift your perspective in all of life in a positive direction. And by using your life experiences to consciously co-create your reality with the Universe via affirmations, you invite into your life the elements necessary for success. Use the tools presented here in this chapter to be your best self and attract into your life the relationship and partner you truly desire—and deserve.

As you come to the end of the guided inner work set forth in this book, you come to the beginning of stepping into a more conscious way of relating.

You've done something most won't—you have taken action toward living *not* by subconscious patterns and programming, but by conscious *choice*—with intention. By learning how to make your mind work for you, shifting your perspective from fear to love, releasing the past and forgiving what was, and instilling new habits that will encompass your day in gratitude, you've made major headway on your journey toward self-discovery and self-acceptance.

Take the exercises and practices from this book and let the lessons guide you in life and love.

TIPS

TO HELP

YOU

STAY IN A

ROMANTIC
RELATIONSHIP

Tips to Help You Stay
in a Romantic Relationship

I've included this section for those who are currently involved in romantic relationships. Successful romantic relationships are only successful because people work their butts off to stay in them. Even your perfect mate—especially your perfect mate—will pose challenges like you've never experienced before. For it is the role of romantic relationships in life to show us our deepest wounds and bring us face-to-face with our shadows. Finding someone you truly want to journey with is imperative, because when times get tough it is all too easy to find a way out of the relationship. However, it is so important to know that just because you exit a relationship with one person doesn't mean you leave behind your shadow. It comes with you into your next relationship, too. This is not to say that you should stay in a relationship that is not a good fit for your life and for your highest self. But it is to say that if you've chosen to do your work with a companion, you may crave a bit of help and insight here and there. That's what I'm hoping the next section of this book will bring to those in long-term, committed romantic relationships.

On Not Losing Yourself in Relationships

Have you heard of beer goggles? Well, they make them for relationships, too.

The relationship ones have rose-colored lenses, and they only let you see what you want to see for the first, oh, let's say three months if you're lucky.

When you're wearing these bad boys, you're totally blind to the process of your own being melting into another's.

Imagine the Stay Puft Marshmallow Man when he meets his Missus . . . and then they vacation in the Bahamas and boom! The whole beach becomes one big Mötley Crüe hit.

During those first few sticky-sweet months with your honey, both you and your love unwittingly "lose yourselves" in the relationship. You become one big gooey person. And while at first this feels really good, and is even necessary for bonding, if navigated unconsciously this enmeshment eventually consumes your very important, independent self.

So what can you do to avoid losing yourself in a romantic relationship—or even to reclaim yourself from a melty, sticky, marshmallowy relationship right now?

1. Commit fully.

   In order to regain your independence while continuing to nurture your precious relationship, you must create a space of emotional safety for you and your partner. If your partner feels threatened by your desire to become more independent, games and fear might jeopardize the relationship. By verbalizing your full commitment to your partner *prior to making any changes*, you can assist the relationship in growing beyond the point of enmeshment.

2. Both you and your partner must support and inspire each other equally.

Let's say Johnny is super inspired by Annie, and he accepts, loves, and supports her FULLY. But Annie, not all that inspired by Johnny's life choices, shows her support by trying to help Johnny with his life. By trying to help, she is actually NOT being supportive of Johnny at all. And Johnny is not inspiring Annie at all. In this relationship, there is an imbalance of support and inspiration. What's this couple to do? Read on to discover a few awesome solutions for Johnny and Annie.

3. Both you and your partner must keep (or revive) your independent interests.

Go out (or in) and rediscover what in life really gets you going—other than your honey. I like to analyze things from a holistic perspective: mind, body, and spirit.

Mind: Get mental. Not in the British way. But in the studious way. Pick up a book, do the random Wikipedia article thing, or sign up for some online class that inspires you. Get hungry to learn and start self-educating!

By focusing on your mind, body, and spirit, you'll refresh your energetic boundaries, and you'll become all the more attractive in your whole and active self.

Body: Examine the physical aspects of your life and find out what appeals to you there. Do you enjoy getting outdoors? Go for a hike! Ride a bike! Go on a walk!

Do you love going to the gym? Hit up a yoga class solo. Hop into Zumba and get that booty movin'! (Yeah, I'm talking to you, too, guys.)

Spirit: Do some inner inquiry into the strength of your spirituality at the moment. Has it waned since you've been in partnership? If so, start some new nightly gratitude practices. Connect with a force greater than yourself. Get really personal with your love and appreciation for life and all that is.

If both you and your partner choose to follow these steps, you'll soon discover balance in support and inspiration.

When consciously creating a relationship, understand that you're working with three elements—you, your partner, and the relationship itself—each to be respected and honored as interdependent, living entities that need attention and nurturing.

By witnessing these three entities simultaneously as individual elements and as parts of a whole, you create the space for a healthy, thriving romantic relationship. And instead of being "lost" in the relationship, you might very well find a deeper, more vulnerable, more authentic version of yourself you wouldn't have identified without your beautiful partner by your side.

On Hopeful
(and Hopeless) Romanticism

Like most rules of thumb, the 80/20 Principle applies to romantic relationships.

Your dream partner is not going to be 100% perfect 100% of the time. But you will *adore*—absolutely freaking LOVE—80% of who and how they are in the world.

So the question is, do you feel this way about your current romantic companion? If so, then it's imperative that if you're having doubts or difficulty in the relationship, you DO YOUR WORK. Even if your partner is not doing *their* work.

If you only truly dig 20% of your partner's interests, morals, values, habits, behaviors, activities, and emotional/spiritual/mental/physical qualities, and the other 80% is stuff that just doesn't resonate with you, it's time to get practical.

Uniting hopeless romanticism with realism is imperative for a successful romantic relationship.

This does *not* mean you:

1. Bail on being a hopeless romantic and treat your relationship like a business partnership, or

2. Allow your chemistry with someone and fantasy of "what could be" to dictate your future with this mate.

However, it *does* mean you:

1. Find a balance between the two extremes, and

2. Use your mind as the tool it is to differentiate the real gold from the fool's gold, so that you have the opportunity to fall head-over-heels in love with a real gem.

If you've found your gem and you're super into 80% of your relationship with this person, but that 20% is seriously making you question things, *that's totally normal*. What is super important to do is to hire an outside professional to help guide you through this probably *really* frustrating time back into a place that feels empowered, independent, inspired, and complete.

If you're just too deep in the relationship to see things clearly and you're really confused about how you feel about the other person at this point, having experienced eyes on the relationship will help you realize what's true for you. Even though it's easy to take our relationship issues to our friends and get their opinions on things, our well-meaning besties are swayed by their love for us, as well as their own relationship experiences.

It is 100% possible to be a hopeless romantic and a practical partner at the same time.

And you know what? You'll feel so much *safer* when you know from a place of confidence that you can commit to your man or lady and fall crazy in love because this is the person you totally want to be with.

On Fights

It happens to the best of us.

We are all human, and therefore susceptible to having our unconscious belief systems triggered—and who better to do it than our significant others?

It seems that when we are triggered, our first reaction is an emotional response; however, that's not actually the case. The first post-trigger response is a *thought*, and a nanosecond later, the emotion follows. And of course it is the emotion which, unless checked, spills all over our momentary rival.

The following process will give you the tools to take note of your thoughts so you can move toward ridding your relationship of repetitive fights.

The next time you're about to explode at your beloved, follow these steps and come back to your lovely, centered self:

1. Stop.

   Recognize what the person said or did that caused this response, and look at it.

   Just stop and look.

   And breathe.

2. Close your mouth.

   Take another breath. And then excuse yourself. Leave the house or restaurant or wherever you are at that moment, and go outside.

Get into nature if you can. Go for a walk. The negative ions and Mother Earth will work together to help re-center and calm you. Plus, while you're in a state of heightened emotion, your energy is palpable and affects your immediate physical environment. Getting outside gives you the space to be big in your emotions without infusing your indoor sanctuary and peeps with this temporary unsettled energy.

3. Act like a person with schizophrenia.

And by that I don't mean go crazy. Well, I suppose if you have to shout, then go for it. But what I do mean is talk to yourself. You see, your S.O. has given you the opportunity to get to know yourself better, so honor the gift and dive in. Feel the emotions, figure out what the root of those emotions is, and, while walking down the street, talk it out. Whip out your phone and audio-record your thoughts. (I personally love audio-recording journal entries.) Or bring a journal with you, find a nice little spot, sit, and write. Either way, only converse with yourself at this time. In other words, don't call a friend or a mentor, just be with yourself and see what you discover. There's some gold in this experience . . . see if you can find it on your own.

4. Give your partner the benefit of the doubt.

I know, I know; that sounds like a ridiculous request. Because it takes two to tango, right? And they dipped you so hard they dropped you. Their bad. Actually, what's crazy to realize is that your partner is doing the best they can with what they've got. Let's say they just did something you asked them not to do a million times already . . . and it's super important they not do this thing, because when they do, a fight occurs. Well, at this point you have to understand that although it may not seem like it, they really are doing their best. And maybe right now they do not have the capacity to hear what you've been requesting. That can be incredibly frustrating, so it is up to you to figure out a safe, calm, and mature way to broach the subject at a time when your partner is available to hear you. More on this later . . .

5. Think of five things you love about your partner.

   After re-centering and before re-entering shared space, bathe yourself in love for your partner. Recall all the reasons you're with this person. Feel the love. Only then will you be ready to re-engage.

6. Share your process.

   It is important for your partner to know the process you went through internally. Without using blame-based language, clue them in to your emotional world and the lessons you learned from inquiring about the trigger. Own everything. Know that this whole fight was about you, for you, and even when explaining it to your partner, you're doing that to help heal you—which you can also express, if you so desire. Only if your partner is emotionally available will they be able to hear you, but—all y'all with male partners—just note that men will often take in information without responding to it right away, so don't expect your partner to give you any kind of response. Remove expectation completely, and do this for YOU.

7. Create a talk-time ritual.

   Set aside a minimum of one hour each week to discuss communication and needs. Let it be fun. Turn it into a ritual that involves the same practices each time. Create a safe place to communicate and allow for heart-opening. Maybe use the same location each week for this practice. Spread out a blanket. Light a candle or sage. And definitely do these honoring practices each time:

   Before you start the conversation, each state your willingness to take responsibility and to hear the other's needs. Then, take turns telling each other:

- Five things you love about the other person as an individual, and
- Five things you love about how they make you feel.

The goal of this practice is not to be right, but to identify situations that trigger undesirable responses (aka fights), and eliminate the triggers. So bless the weekly ritual, and practice it regularly!

Friedrich Nietzsche said it best: "It is not a lack of love, but a lack of friendship that makes unhappy marriages."

Following these seven steps will help you to create a healthy, fulfilling relationship free of unnecessary, unconscious pain and suffering.

On Navigating Your Energetically Masculine Partner

Masculine energy (sharp, focused, and action-oriented) and feminine energy (receptive, flowing, and calm) are attributes of each gender. When individuals are balanced in their masculine and feminine energies, they operate from their most empowered state.

However, most people are not in balance, and either masculine or feminine energies dominate their lives.

Men whose energy is masculine-dominant seem to have no "sensitive side," and when that side does appear, they have a difficult time expressing their emotions. These men may have a short fuse due to their sharp, focused, linear perspectives.

Women whose energy is masculine-dominant are similar. These women seem emotionally frigid at times; they are action-oriented, and they spend more time focused on productivity and forward progress than going with the flow or relaxing.

In romantic relationships, energetically masculine-dominant individuals tend to place high value on alone-time; they are fiercely independent and usually have projects that require their primary focus.

Masculine-dominant peeps aren't rejecting their partners; they're simply doing what they need to do in order to feel complete and satisfied with their day. However . . .

Their focus on productivity can make their partners feel alone, unheard, and unseen.

If you're in a relationship with a masculine-dominant individual, here are three ways to access their loving side and to attract the attention, acknowledgement, and communication you deserve:

1. When they retreat—whether physically or emotionally—let them.

   By giving them the space to go inside, you're allowing them to get quiet, which in turn lets them soften. Their active minds and ambitious spirits keep them going at high speeds, and when they're in productivity mode, they're in a state of release.

   When they emerge from their state of release, they will have cleared their minds and hearts, and they will then have the bandwidth to focus their attention and energy on you and on the relationship. They want to love you, but they're in a near-constant state of overwhelm, and they are sensitive to your "neediness." When in productivity mode, they are fulfilling their needs, and they will likely perceive any need you express as neediness.

   So at this time, let them be with themselves. This will give them the opportunity to emerge with their needs met, allowing them the availability to fulfill yours. You will feel less alone when your masculine-dominant partner can give you the focused, present attention they give their work.

2. State your needs at the appropriate time.

   Imagine being in a state of high stress and having your loved one approach to ask you for something you simply cannot give at that moment. Think how frustrating it is to feel like you're letting your loved one down.

   This is how a masculine-dominant individual feels when they cannot deliver on your requests. Most masculine-dominant people want to live up to all expectations—in fact, they want to exceed them—and when they are not able to, they respond by being defensive. This is not because they're trying to hurt you, but because they're so disappointed in themselves, and they mask that shame with anger and despondence. On a subconscious level, the masculine-dominant partner is trying to get you to lower your expectations, so that in the future they do not need to bear the weight of failure and self-rejection.

So, when you are conscious of your partner's desire to support you—whether that's financially, emotionally, or physically—you can compassionately hold off on making your requests until an appropriate time for a peaceful conversation presents itself. When the masculine-dominant person is outside of their focused, action-oriented activity, they are more emotionally stable, available, and able to hear from a place of inner stillness.

3. State your desires clearly.

   The clarity of your message is as important as the timing. When you have a budding desire or thought, but cannot yet articulate it, and instead begin to talk it out in hopes that your masculine-dominant partner will participate in helping you gain clarity, your exploratory thought process will typically be met with frustration.

   While your masculine-dominant partner wants to know what you're thinking or feeling, they simply cannot translate the meaning of what you're trying to express. This creates miscommunication which often leads to either fighting, or more commonly, an overriding of decision-making by the male-dominant partner. This is a HUGE issue. When your desires are overridden day after day, week after week, and year after year, you'll eventually miss yourself and your independent choices so much that a break-up will inevitably occur. This type of communication in the relationship is fundamentally unsustainable, but it doesn't have to be this way.

Your masculine-dominant partner is not intentionally overriding your desires; you are just not stating them clearly. While it's your job to figure out what you want, and then clearly state it at an appropriate time, it's also important that your masculine-dominant partner learns to be more aware and considerate of your efforts in communicating your needs and wants.

The best thing you can do if you're with a masculine-dominant partner is to allow *their* inspired action to inspire you.

By diving deep into your own passion projects and finding other people in your life to support and love you, you will bring back an energy to your relationship which will promote expansiveness and freedom.

On Being Supportive

Trying to be supportive and *actually* being supportive are two very different things.

My AMAZING friend, Corey Teramana, defines support as this:

"Support is the process of empowering someone through their own faculties and abilities to accomplish, succeed, and grow. Support doesn't steer someone so much as it aids them to discover their greatest attributes and abilities not actively seen. The major key to support is leaving someone empowered."

So this means that what we *thought* was being supportive was actually really trying to change our partner, which shows a total lack of acceptance of the person we love so much. Oops! Our bad.

In other words, unless they are specifically requested, the following activities are NOT being supportive:

- Making suggestions
- Trying to inspire, correct, or control
- Coddling, doting, or nurturing without invitation
- Psyching, healing, coaching, or managing
- Doing research or solving problems for
- Or any other action we perceive as being "helpful"

So the bottom line is this: if you can let go of trying to be supportive by ceasing engagement with the behaviors listed above, you then naturally drop into a state of true support.

By allowing your partner (or anyone else for that matter) to simply be who they are at each and every moment—even if they're miserable, depressed, lethargic, chronically ill, etc.—you are accepting them just as they are and offering true support.

And from this place, the unhealthy person has the space to change *themselves*.

No one wants to be told what to do, and when an adult is told what to do by a partner, something inside of them rebels like an angsty teen.

So then what *can* you do to help shift your relationship into something you're really excited about? Well, I'll tell ya.

Here are three ways you can show your partner true support starting right now:

1. Give them space—physical, mental, emotional, and spiritual. By giving your partner space, you can help them to feel more independent while reminding yourself that you, too, are an independent being with your own needs to meet. Take some time, step back, and focus on you.

2. Notice when you make a suggestion, try to fix something, or "help" in some way. Then stop. Seriously. Even if you have to cut yourself off in the middle of a sentence or turn your car around in the middle of an errand, *do it*. Don't buy that thing you think they'd like, don't do that thing they should be doing themselves. Don't have that conversation you're dying to have because you know if they just did this *one little thing*, everything would be better. Stop the impulse, and let them be. By doing so, you give them the space to ask for help when they need it, and *then* you can be helpful from a place of consciousness and humility. If this gets too difficult, look for your own support system that can help you stay strong.

3. Reflect on your triggers. Take a look inside and witness which behaviors trigger you most. With this raw emotion in mind and heart, go to a quiet place, set an alarm for five minutes, and with an inquisitive energy, breathe deeply into your lower belly. Count your breaths and let them deepen over this period of time, all while holding the trigger in your consciousness.

Allow what comes up to present itself without judgment. Try not to attach to any feeling or idea too strongly; simply see what shows up. After your time is up, jot down any new thoughts or ideas that give you fresh perspective on yourself and/or your relationship.

By remaining in a space of true support—no matter how difficult it is—you'll find that amazing things can begin to happen.

Sometimes you'll need to stay in that space for a lengthy period of time before the unhealthy person finally decides to make small movements toward health—whether physical, mental, emotional, or spiritual. And it can be difficult to maintain a truly supportive role alone. If you find yourself needing support, definitely be in touch with me and I'll be happy to carve out some time just for you.

On Compromising Sexual Needs in LTRs

Our outer lives are a reflection of our inner selves, and as most humans struggle with maintaining balance on an energetic level, our relationships with others mirror those struggles.

When it comes to sexual relationships with long-term partners, all too often one partner compromises their sexual needs and/or desires more than the other.

Again, this is the imbalance between both individuals being reflected in the bedroom—or wherever you like to get down.

For example, if one person in the relationship tends to lean on the other to meet their needs in daily life, it's likely they'll behave the same way in bed.

In this dynamic, the giver in the relationship will also be apt to sacrifice more in the bedroom. From the perspective of the giver (who tends to be more aware of the issue), it may seem they haven't much say in the matter.

But again, the dynamic reflects the partner's expectation to be the recipient and the giver's expectation to make the sacrifice.

Change the dynamic outside the bedroom, and you'll change the dynamic inside the bedroom. Surprisingly—and fortunately—the opposite approach is also effective. When you change the dynamic inside the bedroom, you help change the dynamic outside the bedroom, too.

Practice the exercises below to balance your relationship and create a more gratifying sex life.

The following are the three keys to having a fulfilling sex life with your partner:

1. You are met

   Wouldn't it be great if you could explore whatever it is that tickles your fancy? Or perhaps you're simply not "in the mood" at that moment, and you'd like that fact to be met with understanding and acceptance—without pressure, resentment, or even a hint of disregard. But it's up to you to state your desires/needs before you're confronted with the situation.

   If you expect your partner not to be disappointed with your temporary sexual disinterest—or on the other end of the spectrum, acquiesce to (or challenge) your secret fantasies—things need to be discussed ahead of time. Which leads me to the second key...

2. Your communication is open and received

   It is extremely important to have conversations about sex outside of sexual activity for at least two MAJOR reasons:

   1) When you're in the midst of craving something different or being unsatisfied in some way, emotions run high. Frustration or anticipation can create a flood of impatience, and when you state a need and meet with rejection in this volatile place, not only do you jeopardize that intimate time together, but you also create a rejection-energy around whatever it is you'd brought up in the first place. This makes the conversation that much more charged later, outside of the bedroom, and creates an unnecessary hurdle in getting that desire or need met.

   2) During the act itself—unless you're totally 100% self-confident and unflappable—when your partner asks for something other than what's taking place, it's all too easy to take the request personally.

The love-bubble pops, egos (and other things) deflate, and emotional separation occurs. When this happens, sometimes back-pedaling seems like the only way out, which invalidates your desires and needs and puts undue pressure on the current moment.

So when you can, in a very gentle, graceful way, select a time when spirits are high and no one else is around to broach this tender topic. Start by letting your partner know how much you love having sex with them, and that you came up with a new idea you'd like to try. Be playful about it. Be on their side.

3. You and your partner take turns discovering individual pleasures

Like I said before, it's likely one person compromises more than the other. This leads to long-term dissatisfaction for both parties, as, in the 21st century, compromising either partner's needs has an end-date.

When your previously over-served partner is ready to sacrifice their pleasure for yours, you know you're in a healthy sexual relationship. To initiate this dynamic, suggest a game where you take turns pleasuring each other. It could be per session (one person gets pleasure and the other one gives, and then it's over), or you could switch it up every few minutes. Just make sure you stick to a regular back and forth exchange to introduce the practice of equal compromise.

These three keys reflect the foundation of a balanced, healthy sex life.

The bedroom is a great place to start balancing the giving/receiving nature of an imbalanced relationship.

When you can 1. set boundaries, 2. speak your desires/needs, and 3. learn how to receive and not just give, you invite into the relationship the potential for deeper emotional, spiritual, mental, and physical connection.

While this avenue of transformation is external, the effects of initiating these conversations and balancing practices are internal. By shifting your outer relationships, you can shift your inner relationship with yourself, building self-trust, self-love, and self-acceptance—in and out of bed.

On Getting Ready to Bail

You're in a long-term, committed relationship and you're totally fed up.

You are on the brink of going completely mad because you're so frustrated with the immaturity and/or inaction and/or lack of consciousness of your current partner. It's like: how can they not see you're nearly ready to bail?

You are so on edge that everything this person does makes you want to scream. You're embarrassed by them in public. You hate who you are around them. And you can't help but fantasize about that hottie down the way because he or she is just so damn *chill*.

If this is the case, you need a wake-up call.

No, not from the hotel room you're fantasizing about committing adultery in (thank God, because little Miss/Mr. Hottie has their buckets of issues, too).

But from me. Right here—right now. But first, ask yourself these questions:

- Do I want to cut my losses and toss aside [x] years with this person just because I'm at the end of my rope?

- Am I really ready to leave them once and for all, or do I want to give this thing one last chance?

- What am I willing to do for my sanity, not to mention for a successful romantic relationship?

If you exit this line of questioning with an uneasy feeling that you might be ready to bail, or with a relative certainty that you would like to see this thing through and give it your best, then good. Read on. And go grab a suitcase.

You may have kids. You may have a 9–5 career. You may have a boss who hates you and just won't let you take time off. You may have no money. You may have no time. But there is one thing I can guarantee you will not have if you continue on in this way:

This romantic relationship.

It is time to unplug. It is time to unwind. It is time to let go of routines, responsibilities, and care-taking.

Your romantic partner is not your problem.

Your problem is YOU.

You miss YOU.

You're craving the ability to dictate your life. You're yearning for freedom from habits and patterns. And you're starving for space and time.

Maybe you have a passion project that is begging for attention. Maybe you have a business that barely gets your attention. Maybe you have a stack of books you've been meaning to get to. And maybe you just need to sleep. Like, a lot.

I can guarantee you one other thing right now, too.

If you continue to neglect what your spirit and sanity are demanding, you (and your relationship with your romantic partner who is feeling the brunt of your burnout) will crumble. It will not be pretty. It will devastate areas of your life you cannot fathom. You will kill relationships, injure innocents, and maim parts of your inner self that can be difficult to restore.

But you have a choice.

And although there might be a million reasons why you cannot take some time away, YOU MUST DO IT. For the sake of your relationships, for the sake of your life as you know and love it, and for the sake of your highest self.

Pack a bag and take some time for yourself.

The boldest thing you can do is honor your truth. And if you feel like you're on the verge of a break-up or break-down, go away. Take seven days MINIMUM. Make it happen.

Take a break from life as you know it.

Go hole up in a hotel. Or a motel. Or a hostel. Or through couchsurfing.org if you must. But go take some time to yourself to dictate how each day unfolds without the responsibility of tuning in to the needs of others—without the demand to care for or pay attention to anyone but yourself.

Go be ALONE.

Take some time to sleep first. Then eat what makes you feel good. Be still. Be silent. Write. Read. Cry. Laugh. And be free. Work on your passion project. Pay attention to what you want when you want it. Unplug from social media, turn off your phone, and just be with YOU. And if you find a hottie while away, don't engage. Avert your eyes; be a nun for a week.

Reset yourself and you will reset your life.

Your loved ones will thank you. Your career will thank you. Your partner will thank you. And most importantly, you will thank yourself.

I know change can be difficult, but if your soul is screaming for this, pay attention. Face the fear, and take a leap of faith.

TIPS
TO HELP

YOU
LEAVE A

ROMANTIC
RELATIONSHIP

Tips to Help You Leave a Romantic Relationship

And sometimes you just need to break up and break down, all to break free from the habits and patterns keeping you stuck in an unfulfilling relationship and life situation.

As I said before, if you're preparing to leave your relationship, know that you're not leaving behind your shadow—only the reflections of your shadow-self that your partner is bringing to light. So while it may be best to remove yourself from a sticky situation, one that feels like a boulder weighing you down, you can remain thankful for the opportunity your partner has given you. Now that you're aware of some of the not-so-pretty parts of yourself, you can take the time to give them the TLC they need to transmute and transform, so you don't unintentionally bring those darker parts of yourself into your next romantic relationship.

In the next section, we'll explore some ways to tell if it's time for you to transition into a life of singlehood. Mostly, we'll focus on whether or not your relationship is holding you back from pursuing your passions and dreams, and what to do if that's the case.

If you feel any resistance to reading this at all, I encourage you to take courage and press on. Because this last section could be the key to your deepest, most fulfilling lesson in love.

How You Know You're Using Your Relationship as a Crutch

As Marianne Williamson says, "Our deepest fear is not that we are inadequate. Our deepest fear is that we are powerful beyond measure. It is our light, not our darkness that most frightens us."

In 2007, it became obvious to me that I was using romantic relationships as a crutch, a way to avoid the very important self-gratifying play and work I needed to do. I was heartbroken—but I was also able to see clearly that I'd been sacrificing my creative time, choosing instead to hang out with the person I was madly in love with and watch TV shows.

Even as a teen, I spent hours and hours in front of the television, watching my brother and his adorable friends (one of whom I had a crush on) play video games. What a mind-numbing activity. But I did it so I could spend time with the people I loved.

While the crutch was affecting relationships of all kinds, it was especially noticeable and debilitating in the area of romance.

How frequently do you find yourself doing something you don't want to do just to be around someone you adore?
That last time you were single, did you feel exhilaratingly free? If you look back at that time, do you watch yourself taking leaps and bounds toward your dreams?

If you answered "no," let me clarify the definition of single so you can see if you've ever been single: To be single is to be without *any* love interest, crush, flirtation, or *distraction*.

Let's say you've broken up with someone. Did you suffer the heartbreak feeling, then immediately divert your attention to what felt like a "safe" person to fall for? Or perhaps you redirected your attention to a multitude of people, riding high on the feelings of adoration and acceptance from others. God, it feels good to stroke that ego after the dissolution of a romantic relationship. Trust me, I'm all about getting in a little ego boost here and there. But notice where that takes you.

If you allow the ego boost to become more than a momentary high—if you allow the flirtation to become your next relationship—you've never given yourself a chance to focus on you. You've directed your energy and focus outward because at this moment, inside feels like pain. So it's easier to look outward and feel good, but in doing so, you miss the opportunity to grow up in your emotional body and move toward your purpose from within. When you're in a romantic relationship, do you find yourself taking an interest in your partner's stuff, but knowing that the attention isn't reciprocated or feels feigned? When you want to share what you're doing, do you see your partner's eyes glaze over and their mind totally disengage? Maybe instead of pressing on, you stop and refocus on them because it feels better to have them engaged than it does to be seen.

Important note: *This is not a healthy relationship dynamic.*

Okay. Now, what do you do with that?

First off, why is it happening? It's because in some ways, for a period of time, it's easier to support someone else on their path than it is to move powerfully toward your own life's mission.

Let me say that again. It's easier for a period of time.

But not forever.

We talked about this before. You can only stifle who you truly are for a short time. If you're the only person inspired and engaged in your partnership, it's not going to last long, and if it does, it will crush your soul. You know this. You might even be reading this because you've either experienced this before or are experiencing it now.

Don't crush your soul.

Don't dim your own spirit to try to ignite the light of another.

I don't care how much potential that person has. He or she is *not your person* if this relationship dynamic is present. I know this because he or she is not the person reading this book, and you are. You cannot change your partner—and when you try to, you repel that person further from you. This is your spirit's attempt to create the necessary distance from a situation that is holding it back. Locking it away. Weighing it down so hardcore that sometimes you feel like you're bound to a boulder, and without the relationship, you know you would *soar*.

Have you ever let yourself soar?

How To Get Out of a Relationship That Is Weighing You Down

Let's say you're watching your momentum in life slide to a grinding halt because you've taken on the responsibility for the success of your romantic partnership. Maybe you want to make it work, so you're trying and trying and giving it your all, but deep down you know that if this person doesn't step up and show up, you're going to bail.

Let's say you feel this fire, this drive, and you might not even be sure what the direction of this passion is, but it's there. You've got energy to release into the world, doing something bigger than yourself, working on a mission that involves a global dream of peace, but that also supplies you with the riches and success you *know* you're worth. You know you're meant for greater things than what you're doing right now, and you see your relationship as what's holding you back.

You have two choices.

1. **You can stop taking emotional responsibility for your partner, and create an emotional boundary that allows you to be true to yourself.**

This is an extremely healthy way to operate. When you don't allow your partner to stand in their emotions—when instead you try to take those feelings on yourself—you're robbing your partner of their own opportunities for spiritual and emotional growth. You're putting yourself in the role of enabler and parent.

We went to our parents to make things better. We asked them to hold our emotions for us when they became too painful. When it was time to grow, to suffer pain in order to stretch into new versions of ourselves, our beautiful parents might have held us so we could walk that journey; they might have coddled us, enabling us to develop later; or they might have shoved us off so painfully that we shut down instead of growing up. But regardless of how your parents handled your pain, one thing is certain: if you are a parent to your partner more of the time than not, you're creating an imbalanced relationship dynamic. And that holds you both back from that awesome, soaring feeling of freedom.

If your partner is coming to you and trying to hand you their emotions on a silver platter, using puppy dog eyes or blaming talk or anger or judgment or turning you into a perceived aggressor so they can be the victim, and you're still in the relationship, *you have taken on their emotions and betrayed your own.*

Stop doing that.

Your must remember that *you are not responsible for the way they feel or interact with the world around them.* And, *you cannot change them EVER EVER EVER.* Just because you can see what they "should" do in order to feel better does not mean 1) it's your job to express it, 2) they should actually do it, or 3) you need to stick around and wait to see if they actually make those changes you perceive as their path to healing.

The longer you give your precious time on earth to the writhing and dissatisfied emotions of another, the less time you get to achieve your dreams and become the person you know you're meant to be.

Stand in your own emotional body and let your partner stand in theirs.

When you make this energetic and emotional transition, your partner will either take the invitation and stand up on their own, meeting you in this new, empowered, whole space—or they will crumble and writhe, and then go find someone else to dump themselves upon so they don't have to take responsibility for their own emotions.

By the way, don't blame your partner for this dynamic . . . because we're looking in another mirror here.

You called this relationship in and you, too, did not want to take responsibility for your own emotions and stand in your own strength. Until now. That's fine. Don't beat yourself up. You've been doing the best you can with the tools and awareness you've had along the way. Now it's time to recognize the dynamic and make a change. To shift into the empowered person you know you are. But you might be so at the end of your rope that it feels impossible to alter that dynamic in your current relationship, which brings me to the next option.

2.   Break up.

If you don't feel you can stand in your own emotional body without leaving the relationship, then leave the relationship.

Short and sweet. Or bitter. Sour. Spicy. Whatever flavor of breakup you need to experience, serve it up and dive in. It's painful and it may feel even more soul-crushing than staying stagnant in the relationship itself, but you're finally giving yourself permission to contract, and contraction is part of the expansion and growth process—it is the ebb to life's flow.

How to Stop Using Relationships as an Excuse for Not Following Your Dreams

Back to you.

If you find yourself feeling like you're destined for greater things—like you have a bigger purpose here in life, whether you know what it is or not—and you also find that you're giving yourself over to relationships time and again, you need to face the fact that you're likely using those relationships not only as a point of self-growth, but also as a distraction from shooting for the stars.

We're only given a limited amount of time on earth. My deepest desire for you—the reason I'm writing this book—is that you don't someday wake up on your deathbed wondering what the fuck you did with your life.

We can spend our entire lives hopping from one relationship to the next and never giving ourselves the time to explore our biggest dreams, because it seems like it's safer to grow from relationships than from propelling ourselves into the wild unknown and facing rejection of ultimate proportions.

Here's the kicker.

What you're unconsciously doing when this happens is picking "safe pain." Think about it. At an early age you learned how to cope with a certain type of relationship pain. Maybe it was rejection, maybe it was abandonment, maybe it was feeling like you didn't meet the standards of others. Fill in the blank.

Whatever this recurring childhood pain is labeled, it's something you know how to navigate and handle without totally breaking apart.

What's NOT safe pain is unknown pain.

Pick a different type of pain from the list above (rejection, abandonment, etc.). Think about dabbling in that. Or better yet, imagine what would happen if you did leave the relationship dynamic you've found yourself in time and again and picked a *totally different kind of relationship* to be in. Better still, consider spending some time with yourself, pushing out into the world in the direction of your dreams.

It takes an enormous amount of strength and vulnerability to choose what the possibility of new, unknown pain over familiar pain. You know you can handle familiar pain, but you don't know how you're going to handle unfamiliar pain. And that is scary as shit.

This is why we repeat unwanted relationship habits and patterns. We think it's because there's more lesson in there for us, but that's not it. It's because there's more safety in the familiar—even the painful familiar—than the unknown.

You're still choosing to feel safe.

I can tell you from experience, the safest feelings don't come from enmeshing yourself with another human being. They come from learning to having your own back, standing true in your authenticity, and projecting forward in the direction of your dreams—and throwing caution to the wind.

If you feel you've got bigger things to do, if you think you're here for a higher purpose, but you've been stifling your life's passion for the sake of your relationship, then know this:

If you break free from that dynamic and venture out, exposing your truest desires for your life and for the world, making yourself vulnerable, baring your soul, *and then you fall*, you're going to feel so *much better* than if you didn't get any height at all.

It is safer to fall and fail, having shot for the stars, than it is to remain writhing in mediocrity.

Final Thoughts

Finding a person you are inspired to create a successful romantic relationship with is like taking your first step down a long, windy path full of unknown obstacles scattered about patches of idyllic scenery. If you've chosen your companion with a balance of romance and realism, you have the magic seeds that can grow a dynamic, fulfilling relationship.

But *finding* that person can also be a journey in itself. Louis Pasteur said, "Fortune favors the prepared mind." So instead of spending your time seeking out "the one," take that time to nurture and grow a relationship with yourself—to prepare your mind, body, and spirit for luck, fortune, and love. That's applicable whether you're currently in a relationship or not. You can always practice self-love and self-care, creating boundaries against relationship dynamics that do not serve who and how you want to be in each moment.

To prepare yourself for a successful romantic relationship, do your inner work.

Take the lessons in this book and run with them.

Go far beyond what I've offered here.

Dive deep into your self-acceptance journey—hire a relationship coach, self-reflect, and use your relationships and surroundings to learn more about your inner world.

Witness the life you're calling in.

Realize it is a reflection of where you are on the inside.

Then shift from the inside out and create the reality you truly want to live.

About the Author

Emily Rose is a bestselling author and breakup coach. Her deepest desire is to help people hone in on their passion, remove distraction from their mission, and grab life by the horns.

Hopelessly romantic yet fiercely independent, she's developed her coaching practice to helping you have your cake and eat it, too. She will help you to thrive in your personal freedom while still honoring your desire for meaningful partnership.

Find out more at **emilyrosecoaching.com.**

CPSIA information can be obtained
at www.ICGtesting.com
Printed in the USA
LVHW042247100119
603542LV00019B/1027/P